Magic within Me

Unlock the magic life has to offer

Magic within Me

Unlock the magic life has to offer

Authored by
Preeta Sanjith

Disclaimer

This book has been published with all reasonable efforts taken to make the material error-free after the consent of the author. This book is sold subject to the condition that it shall not, by way of trade or otherwise, be lent, resold, or otherwise circulated without the copyright owner's prior written consent in any form of binding or cover other than that in which it is published and without a similar condition including this condition being imposed on the subsequent purchaser and without limiting the rights under copyright reserved above, no part of this publication maybe reproduced, stored in or introduced into a retrieval system or transmitted in any form or by any other means without the permission of the copyright owner.

Registered Office- 907-Sneh Nagar, Sapna Sangeeta Road,
Agrasen Square, Indore – 452001 (M.P.), India
Website: http://www.wingspublication.com
Email: mybook@wingspublication.com

First Published by WINGS PUBLICATION 2020
Copyright © Preeta Sanjith 2020

Title: THE MAGIC WITHIN ME
Price: INR 249 /$ 9.99
All Rights Reserved.
ISBN 978-81-949161-5-4

LIMITS OF LIABILITY/DISCLAIMER OF WARRANTY

Dedications

I would like to dedicate this book to my mom, **_Mrs. Smita Padhye,_** who passed away this year. She was my strength, my inspiration, and of course, the source of my talent. She wrote beautiful poems herself, but could never get them published, and it was her deepest wish that I would publish my book of poems someday. I will always miss you and love you, mom.

Apart from that, I would like to dedicate this book to my dearest friend, **_Madhumita Nair_**, who helped me transform and made be believe in the magic that life has to offer. This book would never have happened without her presence in my life.

I also want to thank my husband, Sanjith Kumar, for his unconditional love and for encouraging me to pursue my dreams. And my kids for giving me immense joy in life.

Additionally, I want to thank my sister, Jyotsna Chugh, for her unconditional love and support always. I am glad to have you in my life as a steady support system.

Acknowledgement

Every journey like this would have multiple people who have helped, supported knowingly and unknowingly. I would like to thank my family, friends, bosses and teachers who have encouraged me to write. I would like numerous friends who have always liked and appreciated my poems, giving me confidence to keep going on.

But most of all I would like to thank numerous people who have given me so many bitter sweet experiences. It is these experiences which have resulted in this book. I would also like to thank some really special people, who have changed my life and the way I look at it. Thanks for enriching experiences.

I thank the Universe for sending countless miracles and experiences my way so that I could grow and evolve.

Preface

***"The journey to changing your reality
always starts from the inside out."***

A few years ago, I went through an extremely bad phase in my life. It seemed as if my life had collapsed and nothing was going well. Problems kept haunting me one after the other and it seemed like I had no way out of that mess.

But just when I had given up, life decided to surprise me. It revealed to me things that I had always known within me and had forgotten, so I embarked upon a transformational journey, which changed everything for the better.

This is not just a book of poems, it's the summation of that journey in poetry form. These are my personal experiences and lessons that I have learnt. Every poem was written in a different phase of my transformational journey and holds a special place in my heart.

I have written this book with a hope of you finding the answers that I was once seeking as well as your faith that I have now found. I also truly hope that this book helps you find your way back as I found my way back.

-Preeta Sanjith

INDEX

Section

I

Feeling Lost and
Not Knowing Where to Go

Life was great at one point in time: I had financial abundance, a loving husband, and lovely kids. To anyone watching me from the outside, my life would seem picture perfect. But despite all of this, I was not happy on the inside and a strange restlessness always tugged at my heart. I felt lost and like a misfit many times, and whenever I shared this with anyone, they asked me to brush it aside. And that's exactly what I always did.

Then one day, without any warning, my life came crashing down. It started with financial troubles, but very soon, almost everything came tumbling down like a pack of cards.

I had no idea what went wrong and what I could do to correct this. It was as if my boat was caught in stormy seas and I did not know which way to go. It was when I had almost given up that I met someone who changed my life by sharing her story with me. It was a story of faith, belief, and miracles. She sent me on a beautiful journey inside of me that changed my life forever.

I am sure many of us go through phases in life when we feel as if there is no way out and there is no light at the end of the tunnel. But my personal experiences have taught me that the night is usually darkest before the dawn and it is through this stormy path that we discover the power of the divine.

The Lost Wanderer

Lost and battered, I wandered along.
Tired, worn, defeated and forlorn,
I led life as was expected of me,
never questioning or even trying to break free.

Then why did life play such games with me?
Why did I feel so burdened and wanting to flee
I wandered with questions burning in my mind.
Answers to them, I was determined to find.

My soul was traveling on treacherous roads,
taking me towards realms mysterious and unknown.
I wandered for days, months and years,
hoping that the cobwebs in my mind would clear.

And then, in the midst of wandering, I found myself.
I found my heaven in the midst of life's mess.
Now off-beaten paths seem to beckon me.
I have learned to take pleasure in life's uncertainty.

Every wanderer is not lost or directionless,
because life's lessons are on paths trodden upon less.
We all are wanderers trying to discover ourselves,
but our journey is a destination in and of itself.
Why find a destination when
the journey is so interesting?
So, break free and don't stop wandering.

Discovering the True Me

I am lost and I don't know where to go.
What I am trying to discover; I do not know.
My heart is restless and unsure of the right path.
I can feel a shift as if I am undergoing rebirth.
Life is changing and I feel like a ship without a rudder.
A storm is brewing deep within me.
I am questioning everything about me.

I am lost and I don't know where to go.
What I am trying to discover; I do not know.
Answers are inside me, I know that for a fact,
but it's cryptic like a system that cannot be hacked.
The fog just won't lift to show me a clear way.
I simply cannot hear what my heart has to say.
The harder I try, the further away I go.
Maybe in stillness, my heart will let me know.

I am lost and I don't know where to go.
What I am trying to discover; I do not know.
Fulfillment and lasting joy, my heart yearns for,
something that will take my ship ashore.
It yearns for purpose that I need to live through.
something that feels real and true.
My soul wants me to find the true me,
so it has sent me to this turbulent sea.

I am lost and I do not know where to go.
What I am trying to discover; I still do not know.
Many questions are still left unanswered,
but I know the answers will all come
the moment I surrender.
Life will find a way through these turbulent seas,
and when ashore, I know I will discover the true me.

Breaking Apart or Coming Together

Sometimes everything needs to break apart
before you can create a brand-new start.
My life is shattering and I don't know
or is it changing for the better, steady and slow?
Life is turning upside down;
I feel as if I am zipping around on a merry- go-round.

Strange restlessness has taken over me.
From all the shackles, I want to break free.
The direction seems unclear right now.
I don't know where I want to go and how.
My heart is whispering secrets I should know;
It's taking me on a path where I will grow.
Then why do my fears stop me from going?
Why do I stop my life from freely flowing?

Sometimes everything needs to break apart
before you can create a brand-new start.
My life is shattering and I don't know
or is it changing for the better, steady and slow?
I know that everything will keep changing.
It's not a breakdown, it's rearranging.
My heart beats, in excitement and anticipation.
I don't know what lies ahead, but I'm ready for exploration.

Awakening

Grappling with pain, I struggled along,
losing all my will to remain strong.
Suddenly, when life was about to collapse,
truth was revealed in a blinding flash.

My soul was awakened and it was soaring.
All I needed to know was in my face, staring.
The fog had lifted and the sun was smiling once again.
My soul finally healed throughout all of this pain.

It revealed secrets long forgotten by me.
The knowledge of universe set me free
and was guiding me to grow and learn.
I needed my soul to guide me in order for peace to return.
There is no pain and no fear anymore.
However strong the waves are, my ship will find its shore.

God's Mystical Ways

Dark clouds surrounded me.
I tried to find my way, but I couldn't see.
I wanted to give up and I wanted to let go.
Life was at its all-time low.

I tried to fight my way through the storm.
As much as I tried, I couldn't be calm
and I couldn't feel God's love.
My ship was sinking, and I couldn't find the shore.

I didn't believe in any miracles,
but God's ways are beyond the known
Just when I wanted to let go
and I thought life was at its all-time low,
he showered his love in the form of a miracle.
God's ways are truly mystical.
In his arms, he led me through the storm.
From hardship, I came out unscathed and unharmed.

Every problem has a solution,
so, don't lose your faith and devotion.
God showers his love in the form of miracles.
His ways are truly mystical.

I Found God

When my life was crumbling,
in my prayers I kept calling
I kept calling you again and again,
but you did not come, nor did you lessen my pain.

My misery seemed to never end.
The problems in my life never seemed to relent,
I frantically started to search for you.
I went to temples, churches and mosques too.

I went and prayed everywhere,
hoping that you would hear my prayers.
My search for you became quite frantic.
Chants, hymns, offerings, I tried every antic.

Now, I started to wonder if you were really there.
If you existed, did you really care?
Lost and defeated, I gave up my search.
I did not find you in mosques, temples or church.

So, I gathered my strength and decided to fight,
standing strong for what I thought was right.
That's when I instantly knew:
Within me, I found you.

Lost My Way

In the race of life, I lost my way.
I forgot to hear what my soul had to say.
I trudged along bruised and battered.
My life had fallen apart in tatters.

Nothing seemed to come very easily.
Problems were coming repeatedly.
My inner voice reminded me to look inside,
but as a habit, I brushed it aside.

The voice kept whispering in my ears,
and one day, the truth was very clear:
My purpose was to discover my divinity
through love, kindness, and creativity.

The more I imbibed my divine side,
the more I witnessed amazing miracles in my life.
Strife and problems seemed to fade.
Fear disappeared, I was no longer afraid.
I found my way by going inside.
In the process, I discovered my divine side.

Section

II

Dealing with Pain

I was in so much pain once that I could not focus anything beyond the pain I felt. I was trapped and I felt like a victim who could not escape from my problems. But then, I met Madhu, who taught me to see opportunities in my problems. The moment I changed the way I thought, my challenges magically disappeared. I started experiencing magic that was always there, but I was too focused on my issues to see it.

In our lives, we have always been taught to view hardship as something we need to avoid or work towards not having. Our conditioning is to secure our life so as to minimize the problems in our life.

But no one has ever told us that in that darker side of life, the pain can be beautiful. It's beautiful because, in its absence, we will not grow and learn. It's only when we experience pain or uncertainty that we reach our fullest potential. But we de-risk everything to minimize this pain because that's what we have learned.

If we look at nature, we see a caterpillar going through darkness due to being trapped in a cocoon in order to become a beautiful butterfly and we see coal going through fire to become a diamond. The universe is telling us to embrace difficulty and befriend it.

Every problem brings with it an opportunity to learn and grow and become a better version of yourself, provided you are open to it. We can choose to be victims, or we can choose to view every challenge as an opportunity to improve ourselves.

"Life without problems would be like school without lessons."
- Glory Bamon

Pain – Friend, Philosopher & Guide

Hurt is necessary to help you grow
Failure is necessary to make you know
that we need to lose in order to gain
To learn lessons, you need some pain

In the depth of pain, you find yourself
Pain is a means to an end, not an end in itself
Pain can bring the best out of you
if you don't let it get the better of you
Pain can be your friend; it can be your guide,
provided you make that journey inside

Let pain bring out the strength within you
Let it give you an impetus to start anew
Why do we run away from pain?
when from it, there's so much we can gain?
View pain as your friend and it will help
It will introduce you to your best self

There's No Gain without Pain

Stars can't shine without darkness.
As tough as it may be, charge fearlessly.
Rainbows can't be seen without rain.
The value of joy increases after experiencing pain.

Over your failures, you can weep and cry
or think of the chances you miss when you don't try.
If you want to be classified as the best,
then you sometimes need to go through the worst.

Remember that coal handles stress well.
Become a rare and priceless jewel,
become wiser with every mistake you make,
become stronger with every failure in your wake.
We believe in what we tell ourselves,
so have faith and believe in yourself.

Poetry Born Out Of Pain

When the pain in your heart is too much to bear
and you feel that no one in the world cares,
it's when you touch the deepest recesses of your heart
and you feel that your world is in pieces and falling apart.

Don't let this pain overwhelm and drown you.
Instead, let it define a better version of you.
It is when you feel all tired and worn
and out of the pain that beautiful poetry is born.

Let that poetry flow out from within you,
let it define your purpose anew.
Make it a doorway to your inner self,
let your truth shine bright in itself.

Make this pain your friend and your guide
and use it to dive deep inside.
Amidst this suffering, you will find your heaven.
It will help you fight your inner demons.
Out of pain, let the beautiful poetry be born
instead of letting yourself be tired and worn.

Happiness Follows Pain

There's a beautiful rainbow after the rain,
reminding that value of joy increases after pain.
Bringing hope & smile after heavy showers,
reminding you of the infinite power.

The clouds split into vibrant colours after it rains,
reminding you that the best in you comes amidst the pain.
Telling you to bring the best in you, amidst suffering,
instead of in your grief wallowing.

The rainbow spread across the sky in all its splendor,
teaching you the power of faith and surrender.
There's lots to learn from a rainbow in the sky.
Problems can break you down or make you fly.

Be like rainbow that gives joy to everyone.
Be like the sun that gives light when there is none
There's a beautiful rainbow after the rain.
The value of joy increases after pain.

Pain Is My Teacher

As we go through our lives,
all of us can face some strife.
We get few things right
while some, we get wrong.

We can let this make us weak
or we can learn from our mistakes and be strong.
We are not defined by our success
or even by things that we failed at,
but by the experiences that we learned from.

The past might hurt and it might weigh heavily on your mind,
but the truth is, it's made you what you are today.
So look at past with a fond smile on your face.
Treat it like a teacher whom you want to embrace.

Section

III

Discovering the Power within Me

I was deperately searching for answers at one point in time, but the more I searched, the further I seemed to be from the truth. Then, one day, I understood the truth in a blinding flash. Everything I needed to know was within me, and all I needed to do was to be still and just be. In the calmness of my mind, my heart started revealing the truth that I had always known but had simply forgotten. This truth was buried under years of societal conditioning and beliefs formed throughout my lifetime.

The truth was so simple that I wondered how I ever missed sight of this truth. I was writing a script of my life, creating my destiny with my thoughts and my choices. All I needed to do to change my life was to change my perspective and thoughts.

This seemed so easy, right? But that was amongst the hardest things I had ever done. I stumbled and fell multiple times, but it's as if some divine power wanted me to learn and grow. Every time I fell, there was someone or something that gave me courage to get up and get going again.

When going through hardship, many of us look for external solutions or quick fixes. Although, I am not saying these do not work, because I have tried quite a few of them myself. However, they never seem to have the lasting impact that you want them to have and the problems keep coming back to haunt you again and again.

Every problem has a solution that is within you. All you need to do is shift your focus from outside to inside, and that's when you experience the magic that life has to offer.

Everything Is Inside Me

The questions are within me.
The answers are also within me.
There is infinite goodness within me,
so is there is also a demon lurking within me.

There is despair and sadness inside me,
but there is also happiness that can set me free.
There is kindness deep inside me,
but there is also ego that makes it all about me.

I have choice within me
to decide what I choose to be.
Duality in nature is there to make us realize
that power, in our hand, always lies.
The power to choose, the power to be:
Either to be the worst or best version of me.

Dichotomy within Me!!

I asked for courage in all of my prayers
but when the battle came, I was besieged by fears
I asked for infinite happiness to come my way
but when love blossomed, I drove it away

I asked for abundance to fill in my life
but I gave up at the first sign of strife
I asked for lasting love to always be with me
but fear of pain doesn't set me free
I asked for growth and to feel the power within me
but the first sign of problem got better of me

Every prayer and every wish is always heard
Every wish is granted however absurd
But the form and way can be very cryptic
It's up to you to believe it or to be a skeptic

To realize the light, you need to face the darkness
You need pain so your inner power, you can harness
You can let the pain turn you into a bitter or better you
The choice to decide is always within you

Heart Whispers

The heart speaks in a subtle way,
revealing what secrets in it lay.
It reaches, it whispers, it calls,
but we have no idea at all.

Poetry flows from its very soul,
but we ignore it and let it roll.
We choose to ignore what is inside,
forgetting it's our best friend and guide.

We are not even willing to start
listening to the secrets of our heart.
We are too scared to choose it,
so we often prefer to ignore it.

The heart asks us to choose love over fear,
but this is something we would rather not hear.
What use is the heart, if you do not hear it beating?
What use is this love, if you do not keep giving?

Don't be scared to choose love over fear.
At least stop once and hear what your heart has to say
The secrets are all there right inside you,
so let your heart simply guide you.
Shine with love that's deep inside you.
Let your heart be your friend and guide you.

Bending Reality

All my life, I have believed a lie:
You can't change your reality
as hard as you might try
Circumstances I am in define my life,
my dreams can't survive the strife.

I dream of an abundant life full of glory,
but reality tells me a different story.
The difference between reality and dreams is very stark.
The road ahead seems difficult and dark.

"Change your dreams to fit the reality," they say.
Reality can't change easily, try as I may.
But my heart tells me something else:
If my desire to achieve is deep and intense,
dreams will change and bend my reality.
It's only a matter of eventuality.

Magic Wand

I dream of having a real magic wand
with the power to fulfill wishes at flick of my hand:
riches, health, good looks, charm,
and superpowers protecting me from any harm.

I imagine having the ability to fulfill all my dreams.
There's no limit to what I could think and imagine.
The power to change my destiny at will,
the thought itself brings me so much thrill.

A magic wand might be just a fantasy,
but we all have magic within us in reality.
Our thoughts can truly come alive,
provided you strongly believe.

When, to faith, you open your heart,
that's when the magic of life starts.
All of us have magic wands within us,
as long as we have some faith and trust.

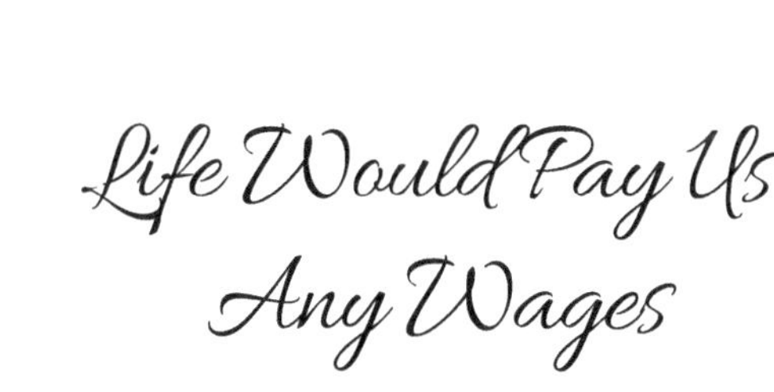

Life Would Pay Us Any Wages

In my thoughts, I bargained with life,
asked it to give me many riches.
But then, I gave up at the first sight of strife,
thinking my dreams are just silly wishes.
Failure seemed to hound me always,
so staying afloat is what I bargained.

Life just gives you what you ask.
So, if you don't get what you have been asking,
for your actions, you must bear the task.
You asked for it, be it abundance or scarcity.

Today, as I am all old and gray,
one thing is as clear as day:
Life is just an employer.
You decide the wages it pays.

Now I realize this with dismay:
life would have willingly given me all I asked for,
just that I chose not to ask for more
It would have paid me any wages I demanded,
if only I had commanded

Section

IV

Being Yourself

Today, I am quite comfortable with who I am and have discovered my true self. But the journey to this discovery was extremely painful. When I was going through the darkest moments in my life, I lost faith in myself, questioning my abilities and my strengths to live life successfully.

Over a period of time, I realized that my idea of the ideal me was based on what was dictated to me by society or my conditioning over many years. I had never given myself a chance to break the shackles of this conditioning and to discover my inner truth. The moment I realized this, I felt liberated and free. I no longer had to live life proving anything to anyone anymore.

If you are going through similar pain, I hope these poems help you make that journey within to find your true, authentic self. Do not be afraid to be yourself... because that's the best you can ever be.

Fitting In

For years now, I have been trying to fit in,
my dissonance hidden behind a fake grin.
People's judgements weigh heavy on me.
Why is it not enough to just be me?

The same path walked down by thousand
Why, within me, does it evoke so many questions?
Sometimes, I feel like I do not belong anywhere,
and I am trying to douse my inner flare.
I feel a fight surge deep inside me,
as if I want to set my inner self free.

I think it's time to reject what is expected of me.
It's time to let go of what others think and just be.
I need to accept my uniqueness
and set parameters for my own success.
For years now, I have tried to fit in
when I should have let my authentic self be seen.

Different Reflections, One True Me

Every time I look in the mirror, I see a different me;
different versions based on expectations people have of me.
Trying to change, to become someone I am not.
In the weight of these expectations, I am caught.

I peer into the mirror trying to find the real me.
I just want everyone to stop expecting and let me be.
The image in the mirror seems to turn into a blur.
"Who am I?" is the question that seems to recur.

Suddenly, the reflection smiles back at me.
Don't change, don't struggle, why don't you just be?
Accept yourself for who you truly are.
Don't let rejections leave a deep scar.

Being yourself is the most awesome thing you can do.
It's letting your inner truth reflect the real you.
Change what you can and accept what you can't.
Love yourself before the world, you can enchant.

Accept yourself for being an awesome you.
That's when everyone will fall in love with you.
Every time I look in the mirror, I just see the real me.
I have learned to accept myself and just be me.

Internal Validation

People can say some really mean things.
It can hurt and bring tears to our eyes
Like cold winds in winter,
words can sometimes cause despair.

Spoken words cannot be a foundation
for your persona's internal validation.
We can't base our accreditation
on someone else's perception.

Imagine how unfulfilling life would be
if you're changing due to what other's think of "me".
I want to build my foundation on solid rock,
not get affected when others mock.
Internal validation is what I seek.
To some, I might seem like a freak.
When my sense of self goes on to rise,
to the negative talk, I become wise.
When I build a strong foundation,
it cannot be shaken by the attacks of a whole nation.

Stop seeking validation from the world outside.
Everything you need is within you deep inside.
All the answers, your heart already knows.
Believe in yourself and your heart will glow.

I Love Being Me

I don't need fancy cars or designer bags.
I will stand out even in my old tattered rags.
My personality doesn't need any accessories.
I will succeed despite of all my adversities.

My radiance doesn't need anything to shine.
It's the glow in my soul that is calm within.
Every problem will only work to better me.
Problems won't weigh me down and I will break free.

The more secure I get with my inner self,
on external factors, I seem to depend very less.
I don't need fancy cars or designer bags.
I will stand out even in my old tattered rags.

Designer dresses and shoes don't define me.
These things are only for the world to see.
What really matters is that I know the real me.
From the shackles of the mind, I am ready to break free.

The True You

You are not the brand you wear,
nor are you defined by being dark or fair.
You are not the shape and size you come in.
You are about your individuality and not how you fit in.

You are not what circumstances make you.
You are defined by how you overpower them to get through.
You are not your success and things you've failed at,
but the experiences that you've amassed.

Don't define yourself by things people think you can do,
because your limits can only be set by you.
Search deep inside and to yourself be true
and then suddenly, you will find the real you.

Be Yourself

If you are beautiful, they will label you as a snob.
If you are not, then you are as plain as a Bob.
If you work hard, then you are a bore.
If you party too much, then you act like a whore.

If you are very intelligent, then you are a nerd.
If you aren't, then you are labelled as a retard.
If you take charge and lead the way,
they call you dominating.
If you don't, then you are dependent
to the point of being irritating.

If you dress modern and fancy,
then you are forward and loose.
If you dress traditionally, you are a social recluse.

They will hate you for what you've got.
They will hate you for what you have not.
You can't please everyone, even if you want.
So, do what you like and your individuality,
be sure to flaunt.

If I Could, I Would Be Me

If I could, how I wish I would be a cloud in the sky.
For hours I would aimlessly soak up the sun and lie.
But then, the wind would dictate where I go,
sending me scampering around when it blows.

If I could, how I wish I would be
a colourful rainbow, spreading joy,
smiling down on everyone, and peeping between
the clouds being all coy.
But my existence would depend on the sun's glow.
Only occasionally across the skies, I would show.

If I could, how I wish I would be a twinkling star,
sparkling and bright,
creating splendor while shining during a dark night.
But then, the morning sun would end my glory.
Every morning would be the end of my story.

Sighing, I think to myself that maybe it's not
so bad being who I am,
even though, at times, it might feel like life is a sham.
Being human allows me to feel a myriad of emotions
and to be a master of my own existence.
If I could, I wish I would remember that
we are God's best creations.
We simply need to take pride in our existence.

Game of Life

We were all born as puzzle pieces of a grand masterpiece,
every bit important and completely unique.
This masterpiece is really wonderful and magical.
Each piece will always fit, even if its change is radical.

But we try to bend our shape and squeeze,
in hopes that we will fit in this masterpiece.
This box comes with no instructions to follow.
The only trick is to try as if there is no tomorrow.

Instead of trying to fit in, we need to enjoy the game,
because every day, the puzzle doesn't look the same.
We are not meant to fit but are unique.
This is a part of the grand design.
So, don't struggle and flow through this game of life.
Don't follow and remember that you are
meant to lead the tribe.

Section

V

Unlocking Miracles in Your Life

The moment I started to believe in myself and my dreams, life started showing me miracles and synchronicities like I had never experienced before. Opportunities appeared out of nowhere and everything started falling into place. But the universe also tested me every step of the way to ensure that I had learned my lessons well and to check if I was persistent in my faith and beliefs.

Every adversity brings with it seeds of equivalent advantage. We can transmute that into physical reality, provided we have an unshakable sense of faith and belief.

Are we ready to put everything we have in stake to achieve what we want? Winners have faith and are willing to risk it all. The higher the risk, the greater the reward. Most people give up when faced with constant adversity on the path to their dreams. But those who persist and persevere are the ones who actually achieve them. The world is full of examples of people who have achieved what they believed in and have even overcome their obvious disadvantages.

But then, what stops you? Nothing but you yourself. Limitations only exist in our minds, and if we believe there are no limitations, then nature will find a way to defy even the toughest adversity. Take Helen Keller for example: She left her mark on the world despite her physical limitation.

Burning desire to the point where it becomes obsession as well as right intention can create miracles. But miracles happen to those who believe in them and who look out for them.

> *"When you believe what you can't see,*
> *you are rewarded by seeing what you believe."*
> – Saint Augustine

That, to my mind, is the power of faith.

Keep Flying...
Do Not Stop Trying

Clear blue skies beckon to me fly.
To float freely in the sky, I want to try.
But when I attempt to, I fall in a heap.
The despondency in me starts to creep.

I decide to give it one more try,
but the bitterness of my failure makes me cry.
Clear blue skies beckon me to fly.
To float freely in the sky, I want to try.

I keep flapping my wings in an attempt to fly.
I dream of soaring heights as, in my bed, I lie.
Every effort I make seems to fail.
The story of my failures will make a sorry tale.

Clear blue skies beckon me to fly.
To float freely in the sky, I want to try.
Despite this, I don't stop flapping my wings.
The hope to soar high is still lingering within me.

Today, I decide to give it a try one more time,
and here I am flying freely and high.
Clear blue skies beckon me to fly,
and here I am because I never stopped giving it a try.

Set the World on Fire

I have my dreams and my desires.
I want to set this world on fire
I know you laugh and mock,
but my dreams, you can't block.

Maybe they seem a little impossible,
but faith and dedication will make them feasible.
I know my path is not very easy,
but this thought doesnt make me uneasy.

Achieving them will make me feel exhausted and creamed,
but I will never let go of my dreams.
Set me free and let me fly.
Even if I fail, let me try.
I have my dreams and my desires,
so let me set this world on fire.

Why Me?

Every time problems hit me,
I asked life, "Why me? Why me?"
when I felt the entire world against me
and from my issues, I couldn't feel free.

Every time my life was in distress,
pain was more than I could even express.
I asked life, "Why me? Why me?"
I lay the blame on everything around me.
It was some kind of escape mechanism for me.

The more the problems, the greater the blame.
I lost my cool and my excuses were very lame.
The problems besieged and didn't let me be.
I asked life, "Why me? Why me?"

Life finally replied and said,
"You need to sleep in the bed you have made.
You are writing the script of your life,
be it happiness or intense strife."

"Yet, you keep asking, 'Why me? Why me?'
I can only serve you what you have asked for.
Responsibility for everything is only yours.
From your problems, if you truly want to be free,
first stop asking all the time, 'Why me? Why me?'
Instead, say: 'It's my life and it's all up to me.'
You have a power to create your reality.
If you can accept the responsibility,
never ask me, 'Why me? Why me?'
Instead, say: 'Change always starts with me.'
Every answer you need is inside you.
Just accept that everything starts and ends with you."

Dreams Come Alive

Dreams have a life of their own.
Dream in such a way that nothing else matters anymore.
When dreams are larger than life,
smaller and pettier seems the strife.

Dream with conviction to make it a reality.
Making them come true is only an eventuality.
Dream in such a way that nothing can exhaust you.
Dream with an intent that resonates with you.

Dream in such a way that you leave all your fears behind.
Dream so that nothing else can play in your mind.
Dreams might test and exhaust you at times.
That's when you need to break all confines.

Dreams have a life of their own.
They come true when nothing else matters anymore.
When your dream is larger than life,
smaller and pettier seems all the strife.

Dreams always come true for those who persist.
Dreams come true when they are the only reason to exist.
Dream away, my friend, and make it come true.
That's when you will be aligned to being true you.

Don't Quit... Follow the Voice Inside You

"Don't quit! Don't quit!" said everyone.
"If you quit, you will always be the failed one."
But my heart sang a different song.
It asked me to quit and not go along.

"Quit and re-discover yourself," it said.
Quit and know that you have a different path laid.
Quit, not because you have tried and failed,
but because this is not your ship to sail.
Quit before you lose yourself to what the world says.
Quit so that you can make your own way."

Quitting at times might be the best way,
whatever the world might say
Your inner voice is always there to guide you,
telling you what's the best path for you.

The Special Spark Inside Me

Deep inside me is that special spark.
But every time, something holds me back,
I let others decide my worth for me.
Trapped in these beliefs, I am never free.
Insecurities and fears take hold of me.
I wonder if someone will see the spark in me.

Deep inside me is that special spark,
but everytime, something holds me back.
Today, I decide that I will decide my own value.
In my abilities and talents, I will believe.

The moment I change my inner story,
life unfolds in all its grand glory.
I realise now that I need to believe in me.
That's when I let my inner talent free.
Deep inside me is that special spark.
I will not let my beliefs hold me back.

Keep the Hope Alive

When the world seems bleak
and there is nowhere to go,
hope is the thing you want to know.

When the world seems too slow
and you don't seem to know,
hope is friend to whom you must go.

When the world has dark hues,
hope will carry you through.
When you are down with broken heart,
hope can infuse a new start.

Hope can fill darkness with light.
It can help provide you respite
Hope is your friend and your guide.
It can help throughout bad times.

When the world seems bleak
and there is nowhere to go,
whatever you choose to do,
never ever let go of your hope

Difficult Roads Lead to Beautiful Destinations

It's easier to disbelieve than to believe.
It's easier to hold grudges than to forgive.
It's easier to be unkind than to be kind.
It's easier to break down during life's grind.
It's easier to criticize others than to praise.
It easier to fear the unknown than to embrace.
It's easier to hate what's different than to love.
It's easier keep the past alive inside than to let go.

Easy options seem to be always calling.
Into their vicious trap, you are always falling.
But what's easy and available at first sight
might not be the option that's always right.

Tough roads might make you uneasy and unsure,
but to be best version of yourself, you need to endure.
The journey to self-growth starts from the outside in.
It involves looking inside you, deep within.

The more you discover, the easier the journey.
You will enjoy the process of self-discovery.
Remember that difficult roads
lead to beautiful destinations,
even though easy roads might offer many temptations.

Power of Faith

Faith is the sun and dreams are moon.
Without faith, dreams will fade away soon.
So, believe in your dreams and have faith.
The reward for patience will be worth all wait.

When you set to achieve your heart's deepest desires,
it brings out your inner passion and fire.
The more you surrender and less you obsess,
the more the journey becomes easy and effortless.
The universe supports you to achieve your dreams,
when you persist despite of all the extremes.

Faith is the sun and dreams are moon.
Without faith, dreams will fade away soon.
Believe that your dreams will come true,
and in the process, you will find the limitless you.

The Voice Inside You

When your inner voice guides you,
it makes sure that, to your dream, you remain true.
Life weaves it's magical story,
and you start feeling it in its full glory.

The universe aligns itself to support you
and miracles seem to happen out of blue.
But the inner voice always whispers in your ear,
yet you downplay it and listen to your fears.

All of us have unlimited capacity,
but towards our dreams, we need to have tenacity.
Magic can happen at every instance
as long as faith becomes a part of our existence.
Believe in good things and magic comes alive.
Even the worst situation, you can revive.

Monster under My Bed

For years now, I have a monster under my bed.
In the creepy darkness of night, it crops up his head,
playing with my thoughts in the shadows of night
and swallowing me in darkness however hard I fight.

This monster seems to take my name,
saying things that keep messing with my brain.
The monster reminds me of all my insecurities;
I feel crippled with all my disabilities.

For years, I have feared this monster under my bed.
Now I realise that it lives in my head.
It crops up its head in the darkness of night,
swallowing me in darkness however hard I fight.

But today, I decide to keep it at bay.
With positive thoughts, I send it away.
No longer do I have a monster under my bed,
because I now have angels guarding my head.

Section

VI

Purpose of Life

One of the biggest questions that hounds most of us or at least a few of us at some point in time is: "What is my purpose? What am I born to do? If life is a series of experiences, then what is the purpose of my life in and of itself?" These questions have hounded me for a long time.

Over the last few years, my search for the answers to these questions has been intense. Then, a few days ago when I was meditating, the answer to this question emerged. It was so simple that I wondered why I didn't realize it before. This realization has changed my perspective.

The reason that we go through new experiences is growth. We need to grow and learn. Life is like a school where we are learning and growing through our experiences. Everyone has unique experiences, depending on the lessons they need to learn. But this growth is essential. It's essential for us to achieve our purpose.

And what is this growth about? Is it about our career or about our personal development? It is growth to realize that we need to reach our inner Divinity. To do this, you need to be loving, kind, empathetic, creative, and expansive in your thought process. Each life experience is just an attempt to teach you this. This is what life is all about, which makes you a ray of sunshine for those around you.

And it's so simple because we have our internal GPS to guide us through these experiences. Anything that doesn't feel good can't be good and anything that makes you happy and positive is the right thing to do. I wonder why we complicate it so much.

Purpose of Life

My heart kept searching for something.
So, every time, I kept trying new things.
I thought money would fulfill my longing,
but that didn't seem to satisfy my yearning.

I decided to chase success and fame,
thinking that would end this game.
But the harder I tried, the more it kept eluding.
I didn't know what I was missing.
A strange sense of restlessness came over me;
I tried hard to break the chains and be free.

Then, in quiet moments, my heart spoke.
Secrets buried inside were revealed
The truth of my life was unvieled.
My purpose was to freely give my gifts;
It was when my soul made an eternal shift
and connected me to the divinity within me.
My purpose was to be the best I could be,
to give without any expectations and reservations.
That's was the intent of divine creation.

Unknown Path

Have you every felt some pain or ache
while thinking about the unknown path you didn't take,
where the destination was not clear
and you held back due to your fears?

This unknown path, you don't know where it might end.
But your limitations, you can never transcend.
The path promises many mysterious delights,
but letting go of fears has always been a tough fight.

It's an unknown path where you must tread alone.
However confused you may be,
you must do this on your own.
You try to blurr the noise from your head
because the unknown fills you with dread.
The path keeps calling out to you all the time,
hoping you will hear the call sometime.

An unknown path with a destination all blurred,
creating a tug in your heart that you've never felt before.
Have you every felt some pain or ache
while thinking about the unknown path you didn't take,
where the destination was not clear
and you held back due to your fears?

The unknown path keeps beckoning me to walk through.
Today, I decide to overcome my limitations and let go.
The destination to this path, I do not know.
But my heart tells me that onward, I must go.

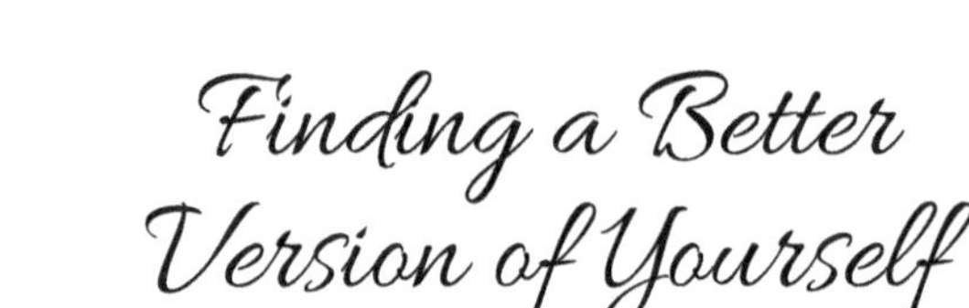

Finding a Better Version of Yourself

In the journey of life, we all get bruised.
While dealing with pain, our energy gets diffused.
We all have things that have left us broken
and wounds that are better left unspoken.

Tackling this is the complicated part.
So often, we bury it deep in our heart.
But if we want to feel free and light,
then every cell in our body needs to fight.

We must free our soul from the prisons of these wounds
from the past, then we would no longer be bound.
We must heal our pain so that we feel complete and well
and heal every part of our mind that isn't in good health.

As we heal, we discover our true self
Universe conspires to give us all the help
We all have things that have left us broken
and wounds that are better left unspoken.
We shouldn't judge, be harsh or unkind.
Instead, a better version of ourselves,
we should try to find.

Scarred yet Beautiful

Beautiful moon in the dark night sky,
so close yet so far up above and high,
amidst so many stars, you stand apart.
Despite your scars, you make your mark.

You go through phases, but never cease to shine.
And then you're back to being a full moon every single time.
You tell me that I am unique despite my flaws,
that this sad phase will lead to happiness, as is the law.
You teach me to shine against all odds.
Beautiful moon, of the dark skies, you're the lord.
You are my guide, teacher, and friend.
To my thoughts, your ears, you lend.

Beautiful moon in the dark night sky,
so close yet so far up above and high
amidst so many stars, you stand apart.
Despite your scars, you make your mark.

Everything Is an Illusion

Is the world what you really see?
Or is it an illusion created by you?
You see the world through your lens,
using your perception to make sense

Everything you see is a figment of your mind,
all of us living in a different reality each time.
You see the world in your own unique way.
When others dont agree, you feel dismay.

What you think is what you project.
Everything else, you seem to reject.
You blame, you fight, and you judge others,
but to understand their view, you don't bother.

It's all an illusion called reality.
Thoughts differ and there is no parity.
If you understand this, then you'll let others be,
because they see the world differently.
Everything is an illusion created by your mind.
Go within yourself and your reality, you will find.

Child Within Me

Trapped deep inside me is a little child,
wanting to break free and run wild.
This child sees the world with eyes anew.
It enjoys first rain and morning misty dew.

No limitations and no chains bind me.
No worries or stressors bog me down.
I feel joyous and carefree.
This child often peeks from within me,
wondering when I will let it free.

It comes out every once in a while,
making those little moments worthwhile.
It teaches me to smile and let go,
enjoying life in its glorious flow.

But I fear the world might judge and mock,
so this child remains under a lock.
Trapped deep inside me is a little child,
wanting to break free and run wild.

Section

VII

Finding Happiness

People spend years trying to find happiness. However, it eludes them because happiness isn't a destination, it's a journey in and of itself. Happiness is a way of life and not just some moments when you enjoy it.

Over the past few years, I have experienced tremendous personal growth, but the path to this was through some seriously bleak and unhappy moments. This journey has been from the inside out and has completely transformed the way I think about life. I've spent years trying to find happiness and peace outside of myself. I also kept on chasing goals and material success, but I didn't find what I was searching for. I got tired, stopped my search, and looked within me. And that's exactly when I found all the answers that I was seeking...

Lasting happiness can come only when you connect with your inner divinity. And the only way to connect to it is by embodying the virtues of the divine: being loving, kind, creative, appreciative, abundant, and receptive and expansive in your thought process. The moment you deviate from these, you disconnect from your source and happiness eludes you.

Do things that bring joy and fulfillment from within, and you'll know you are connected to divinity. The game of life is simple if you play by the rules.

The Race of Life

I kept on chasing life in some kind of race.
I didn't want to slow down and lose my pace.
I got so caught up in chasing that I seemed to forget
what it was that I started out to get.

In this process, life seemed to have left me behind.
I found treasures of the world, but had lost my mind.
Exhausted and tired, I crumbled down completely.
The signs were all there, and I ignored them repeatedly.

Now, I am learning to walk all over again.
Inside me, an entirely new journey has begun.
Today, I am no longer running any race.
Nor am I worried about losing my pace.
The unraveling of life is peaceful and slow.
What my soul wants, I take time to know.
No longer do I seem to lose my mind.
Life is no longer left somewhere behind.
Happiness and peace have made their way back to me
when I stopped running and decided to just be.

What Is Happiness?

Happiness is sunshine coming through the window.
Happiness is humming along to a song on the radio.
Happiness is the first morning cup of tea.
Happiness is the sound of the splashing sea.

Happiness is licking melting ice cream.
Happiness is doing crazy things.
Happiness is getting wet in the first spring rain.
Happiness is dancing in it as if you are insane.

Happiness is building sandcastles.
Happiness is letting go of worthless battles.
Happiness is spending time with loved ones.
Happiness is jumping over the bouncing waves.
Happiness is exploring your mind's hidden caves.

Happiness is the smile you share with a stranger.
Happiness is when, outside of comfort zone, you venture.
Happiness is not in those big lofty goals you achieve.
Happiness is found in these small moments you live.

Seeking Happiness

Happiness is what our soul seeks,
so why do things where unhappiness creeps?
Instead, do things that make your heart feel joyful and glad.
Why surround yourself with things that make you sad?
Find your happiness, and you will emit
the energy of radiance.
That's when the universe aligns itself to shower its abundance.

Leave all those negative thoughts behind.
Empathy and forgiveness alleviate your mind.
The game of life is really simple and very clear.
Play it by its rules, and towards your rewards, you will steer.
Life is truly beautiful and full of miracles.
All you need to do is break your mind free of those shackles.

Face of God

If God had a face, I wonder how it would be?
I start thinking and let my imagination run free.
God would look like a great artist, I think.
After all, he created such a wonderful world in a blink.
His creative energies can be seen in everything,
from snowy winters to beautiful springs.

God is incredibly beautiful inside out.
Look around you and know this without a doubt.
God looks like a person who is extremely kind.
Someone who creates can't be any other way inclined.

God would probably look like a mother.
Can a life-giving source look like any other?
God is full of love, creating and nurturing life
and loving others even when going through strife.

God is like richest businessman,
always abundant and having grand expansion plans.
But above everything, I think God looks like me.
After all, I am an integral part of source energy.
Within me, I have creativity, love,
kindness, and abundance.
All negativity is simply unnatural and redundant.

Section

VIII

Power of Gratitude
and Surrender

The key to living a fulfilling and happy life are two simple pillars which you need to base your life on: gratitude and surrender.

When they announce a bonus in your office, aren't you happy because it isn't something that is taken for granted? A salary is expected and doesn't make you feel happy, but a bonus makes you happy. We should think of life exactly like this: everything is a bonus. If we consider everything in life as a bonus, we will be forever grateful for whatever we have and stop focusing on what we don't have.

Gratitude is the only thing that can produce deep joy because we realize that God is working with us, even through our problems. Similarly, surrender is the only way to make life happen through you. When you surrender to the divine power and accept that it knows exactly what you need and will guide you through hardship, miracles can happen. Does this mean you stop all action? Of course not, but you surrender the outcome of the process to the divine. Accept every outcome as being the best one for you and an opportunity to reach your inner divinity. That way, there would never be a reason to be unhappy.

"The moment of surrender is not when life is over, but it's the moment life actually begins."
- Marriane Williamson

Prayer of Gratitude

For years now, I have been asking and asking.
To the divine power, I have been praying.
I have asked for things I want to have
like a perfect life and abundance that I crave.

But God doesn't seem to hear my prayers.
I wonder if the requests go through many layers.
To my questions, I seek answers that are clear.
Teachings of religious gurus, I hear.

They keep telling me to pray more intensely,
but a divine blessing is still quite a mystery.
Tired and worn out, I am about to give up.
To my miserable fate, I might as well succumb.

In all this despair, I hear the divine speak to me.
Now I know it has always been talking to me.
I stop praying for my wants and desires
because the divine already knows all that is there.

My praying is completely redundant,
showing my lack of faith in divine abundance.
So now, I just send a silent prayer of thankfulness,
knowing that divine energy will do the rest.

Don't Pray, Just Thank

God who made these oceans and seas
will surely, without saying so, understand me.
The hands that created every small thing
will surely know my deepest desire and wish.

Praying for things that I need and want,
talking about my faith, which isn't staunch.
If I truly believe in the divine presence,
then I know that I have the same essence.

The need to ask becomes redundant.
Because the divine always wants me to be abundant.
Then, what does one pray for, you might ask—
if really, in abundance and success, you need to bask?

Gratitude for things seems to be the only way.
Because lack or wanting it doesn't convey.
When I feel thankful for the divine presence,
there is no feeling of lack or absence,
so I send a silent prayer of thankfulness
and let the divine energy do the rest.

Meaning of Life

Life is a journey, some say.
We need to keep walking, come what may.
Some say life is like a river flowing.
Whether there's sorrow or happiness, it keeps on going.

For others, life is like a game that they need to win.
Their success defines their entire being.
For others, it's like a sprint during a marathon;
They don't ever stop and just keep going.

What is life really all about, I wonder?
To this mystery, everyone wants an answer.
But isn't life and myself the same?
It's not a journey or a game.
Neither is it a river flowing.
Nor is it race where you keep on running.

I am life and life is me,
and this knowledge sets me free.

Power of Surrender

Are you tired of struggle and strife?
Are you thinking about how challenging life is?
Maybe it's time to rest and let go,
surrendering to life's grand flow.

The moment you let go and surrender,
amazing miracles, the universe will render.
Let go of your pain and fear.
The moment you surrender, the path will be clear.

Place your worries in arms of power so strong.
When the problems vanish, you will
wonder what took you so long.
When life seems tough, you should know
that the best thing you can do it surrender and let go.

Surrender is not quitting or not trying;
It simply means you no longer worry.
The outcome, whatever it might be,
will happen for the best.
Let the divine power work its magic and do the rest.

Do the best you can and then simply surrender.
Stop worrying about the outcome and don't ever wonder.
The universe will deliver the best outcome to you.
Surrendering is all that you really need to do.
The power of surrender is quite grand.
With faith so strong, no problems can stand.

Section

IX

Dealing with Death

I think one of the biggest fears we have in life is death. Death invokes emotions in us that life never can. But isn't death an eventuality that we all will face one day?

I would like to think of death as a journey into another realm and another reality. Maybe it's a higher school, where I would continue my lessons and growth in some other form. Why should I fear or lament over death, when it is simply a merging into divine energy? This is the ultimate wish and destination of every soul, and maybe the beginning of a new and unknown journey to learn new lessons.

I recently lost my mom and even though it was tough, accepting that her physical presence will not be with me anymore was difficult. But knowing that the soul is eternal and our paths will cross again in the journey of life gave me comfort to deal with this grief.

As I come to end of this book, I would like to leave a few thoughts on how we view death and maybe help you deal with the death of your near and dear ones.

Death: The Ultimate Destination

Why fear death when deep inside us, we know
that it's a natural destination to life's flow.
The same hand that made flowers and trees
will guide me to where I really need to be.
The same power that made oceans and seas
will surely know how to steer and guide me.

The loving hand that made the desert and sand,
in this unknown realm, will surely hold my hand.
The hand that made me is loving and kind,
then why do I cry and look behind?

Why shed tears when there should be celebration?
Death is the journey of a soul's liberation.
It's a manifestation of the soul's deepest desire:
to be one with the divine energy and power.

I do not regret or fear death anymore.
This is where my ship meets its shore.
It's not an end, but just a new start,
so let it not invoke any fear in your heart.

A Pot of Ashes Is All that Remains

A pot of ashes is all that remains.
It's a reminder of a life that was once there.
All the desires, all the wishes…
Everything is down to ashes.

Ego, anger and anguish, you felt.
Somehow, all seems to be in vain.
There are no riches and no people that you can carry with you,
except for lessons that you came here to learn.
Yet, you remain entangled in things that don't matter,
when all you can do is learn lessons and be better.

A pot of ashes is all that remains.
It's a reminder of a life that was once there.
As I let your ashes wash away in the sea,
I know you will always live inside me.
Deep down within my heart, I know
that your love will create a glow.

In My Memories, You Live

My eyes crave to see you around.
My ears crave to hear your sound.
I long for your gentle pat on my head.
I wish I could have told you all things that had gone unsaid.

I wish I could see you for one last time.
I wish that, with you, we had some more time.
But you are gone far away, never to come back.
My mind keeps going into a flashback.

Memories of you are all that are left with me;
They will always be there bringing a smile to me.
As I close my eyes and start to dream, I find you.
You're happy and smiling in some place new.
Your memories will always live inside me,
prodding me to be the best I could ever be.

You Live in Me

I miss your eyes looking at me with intense love.
I miss your voice reassuring me of your love.
I miss your smile creating a warm glow within me.
I miss your presence in which I could just be.

But I won't let this become a grief inside me,
because I know deep down, you live within me.
After all, I am an integral part of you;
Everything I am is a reflection of you.

I will not let your memories bring tears to my eyes.
Instead, your memories will evoke a fond smile.
All of my strengths have come from you.
I will harness their power just for you.

But I won't let this become a grief inside me,
because I know deep down, you live within me.
You will live through all the things that I do.
In the process of finding myself, I will rediscover you.
You will always live in this world through me.
So today, I choose to be the best version of me.

Now I come to the end of this journey and I hope you enjoyed it. I wrote this book in hopes of answering questions that I was once seeking answers to. Life was very kind to me and sent me answers in the form of a friend who has guided me when I needed it the most. I hope this book can be a friend to you.

As I end this book, I leave a reminder that we are never alone and are always guided and supported, even in our bleakest moments.

God Is Always with Me

When I felt alone, I made you my friend,
for I knew you would never leave me till the end.
I lost my way and I needed a guiding hand.
With you guiding me, in right place, I would land.

When I needed to learn, I made you my teacher.
No one else could help me learn better.
When I needed my parents, I called for you.
No one could care for me better than you.
When my life seemed dull and full of blues,
I knew I could always lean on you.

You are the tiny voice that speaks to me.
You are an integral part of me.
Your loving hand guides me all the time.
You are a friend, teacher, and parent of mine.
I call you by different names.
God, Universe… but all of them are the same.
You always have been a part of me.
All I needed was a vision to see.